Follow

Written by Keith Pigdon

Photography by Michael Curtain

HORWITZ
MARTIN
EDUCATION

Here is the tree
where I play.
Come and see —
follow me.

2

Here is the path
to the tree
where I play.
Come and see –
follow me.

Here is the trunk

of the tree

where I play.

Come and see –

follow me.

Here is the ladder
on the tree
where I play.
Come and see –
follow me.

Here are some leaves

on the tree

where I play.

Come and see –

follow me.

Here is a branch

on the tree

where I play.

Come and see –

follow me.

13

Here is the tree house

in the tree

where I play.

Come and see –
follow me.